Leonardo da Vinci

Karen Ball and Rosie Dickins
Illustrated by Christa Unzner

Art history consultant: Dr. Erika Langmuir, OBE
Reading consultant: Alison Kelly, Roehampton University

Edited by Jane Chisholm
Designed by Michelle Lawrence
Digital manipulation by Nick Wakeford

First published in 2007 by Usborne Publishing Ltd.,
Usborne House, 83-85 Saffron Hill,
London EC1N 8RT, England.
www.usborne.com

Printed in China. UE.
First published in America in 2007.

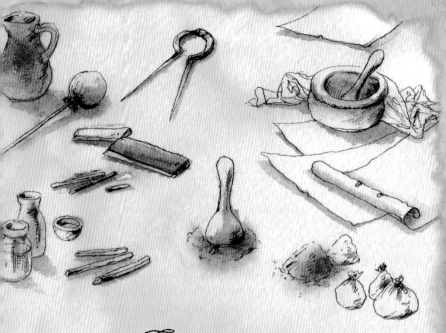

Contents

This map shows the main places where Leonardo da Vinci lived and worked. In his day, Italy was divided into separate states and France was smaller than today.

Chapter 1

Village life

1452-1469

Vinci, Italy

"Leonardo! Where are you?"

The man stood at the top of the chalk path that led the way through the local vineyards to the winding Arno River. He raised his hand to shield his eyes from the setting sun, and called out the boy's name for a second time.

"Coming!" A handsome young teenager with long, curly hair climbed out of the reed beds by the river. This was Leonardo, and the man was his Uncle Francesco – although they seemed more like father and son.

Leonardo's real parents hadn't been married and his birth had been an accident. Still, his father, Piero, had been pleased to have a son and had brought the child to live with him and Francesco in their village house in Vinci. But Piero was rarely home. He was a lawyer with a busy city office in Florence, a whole day's ride away.

So it was Francesco who looked after Leonardo. He taught the boy to love the countryside and all its plants and animals, and tried to answer his endless questions...

Leonardo ran up to his uncle. His feet were soaking wet.

"I see you've been messing around in the river again," laughed Francesco.

"It's not messing around," Leonardo replied crossly. "It's important scientific study!"

"Tell me what you've studied today, then," said Francesco gently.

"Eddies," said Leonardo. "The way that water moves. It's fascinating! It's given me an idea for a water mill. And I drew some of the riverside plants."

Leonardo held up a notebook crammed with notes and sketches of flowing water and flowering plants. The notes were mostly jotted in mirror writing. Being left-handed, he found it easier to shape his letters back-to-front.

As the sun sank lower, Leonardo and Francesco began walking back to their house on the Via Roma, nestling in the shadow of Mount Albano. Leonardo, who was always making up tunes, sang as they walked. Suddenly, he stopped and reached for his chalk. He had spotted a bird rising effortlessly on the breeze from the mountain.

"Look how it soars!" he exclaimed, deftly adding another sketch to his book.

When they reached home, Leonardo ducked his head to walk through the low doorway, while Francesco paused to inspect the garden. To Leonardo's surprise, he found his father inside, leafing through a pile of legal papers. Leonardo greeted him politely, wondering why he was back from the city.

The village of Vinci, deep in the Italian countryside, where Leonardo grew up

Piero coughed. "I've come to talk about your future," he began. "You have an inquisitive mind. Now it's time to make a decision. Either you continue at school or..."

Leonardo couldn't contain himself. "Or devote myself to art? Father, I want to study art in Florence. Please! There's so much I could learn."

In his excitement, Leonardo nearly dropped his notebook. He had heard such a lot about Florence and the astonishing work being done by the city's artists, architects, writers and scientists. These were thrilling times and he wanted to be a part of it... badly.

Piero nodded slowly. "I've already made some inquiries," he admitted. "One of the city's best artists has agreed to take you on as an apprentice – if you're sure that's what you want."

"I am! I am!" Leonardo ran across the room and flung his arms around his father. "Which artist?" he asked.

"The painter and sculptor Andrea del Verrocchio. I've shown him your drawings and he's impressed…"

To read Leonardo's writing, try looking at it in a mirror.

"Just promise me one thing," added Piero.

"Anything!" vowed Leonardo.

"When you start a project, get to the end of it. You have talent, but you rarely finish things. You must learn to see them through."

"I'll try!" Leonardo called, as he raced into the garden to tell Francesco the news.

Piero watched his son's retreating back and smiled. "I have a feeling this could be the start of a great career," he said to himself.

Florence today, with the same
domed cathedral Leonardo knew

Chapter 2
Off to Florence

1469-1481

Leonardo and Piero gazed up at Florence. A
watch tower cast a long, cool shadow over
them and, on either side, the city's tall,
sandstone walls stretched out as far as they
could see.

"Fifty thousand people live inside these
walls," said Piero, as they joined the crowds
jostling through the gates.

"So many!" thought Leonardo. He had
never seen anything like it.

Inside the walls, Piero led the way through a maze of narrow streets. They passed dozens of shops and workshops – tailors, weavers, dyers and one shop selling fur and leather. Leonardo winced. He hated killing animals and never ate meat.

Turning a corner, they saw a new mansion being built. Clouds of yellow dust billowed up around the workmen.

14

A passer-by threw a coin into one of the newly dug trenches.

"Why's he doing that?" Leonardo asked.

"It's for good luck," said his father. He handed the boy a coin. "Go on, you do the same. You're at the start of a new adventure – you might need some luck, too!" He watched proudly as his son closed his eyes and tossed the coin into the trench.

At last, they reached a workshop in the
east of the city. Piero gave his son a
goodbye hug. "I'll leave you here," he said.
"This is Andrea's place. Now, you're an
apprentice. Your real learning starts here."
Leonardo hesitated for a moment,
then stepped through the doorway.
He found himself in
a cluttered room,
reeking of varnish.

A boy about his own age was scrubbing a
paint-stained table, while another worked at
an easel. From a corner came the sound of
hammering. One of the boys glanced over.
"Master Andrea!" he called. The
hammering stopped and a burly,
dark-haired man looked up.

Andrea looked Leonardo up and down. "You must be the boy from Vinci," he said. "Leonardo, isn't it?"

"Yes, sir," said Leonardo quietly.

"Well, Leonardo *da Vinci*,* this is a business," warned the famous artist. "Paper's expensive – so if you're going to learn, you'd better learn quick."

Leonardo grinned. "Oh, I can do that," he said. "Just show me how."

The older man smiled. "I think you're going to fit right in," he said, handing Leonardo a stick of chalk. "Start by showing me how well you draw. After all, if you can't draw, how can you begin to paint?"

Days at the workshop passed quickly. Orders for new paintings and sculptures streamed in from the rich people and churches of Florence.

*"da Vinci" is Italian for "from Vinci" – which is how Leonardo would be known from now on.

While Andrea and the older apprentices painted or carved, Leonardo and the younger boys ran around sweeping floors, sharpening chisels, washing brushes and preparing paints.

Ready-made paints hadn't been invented. Instead, lumps of bright substances known as pigments, such as yellow clay or green stone, had to be ground into powder. The powder was then blended with water, and stirred into egg or oil to form a smooth, sticky paste...

Leonardo loved making paint; from lead white to ultramarine blue, there were so many beautiful pigments to try.

Whenever there was a spare minute, Leonardo sketched furiously. Under Andrea's watchful eye, he tried drawing people and drapery. And he worked hard at perspective – the tricks artists use to create the illusion of space and depth in their pictures. Andrea taught him to observe how objects grow smaller and hazier with distance, so he could mimic the effects and make his scenery look just like the real thing.

Several years went by – and still Leonardo had not been allowed to work on any big paintings. One afternoon, he was dreamily sketching an angel when Andrea walked past, carrying a sheaf of drawings for a new order.

"Very good," said Andrea, pausing to admire the angel's delicate features and beautiful curled hair. He clapped a hand on the boy's shoulder. "I could hardly have drawn better myself. In fact, there may even be a place for him in our next painting…"

"At last!" thought Leonardo, grinning.

Andrea took him to the back of the workshop, where a freshly cut panel of poplar wood lay ready.

The panel had been coated with chalk paste, giving it a silky white surface. Andrea had already marked out the main figures. Now, Leonardo added his angel...

21

First, he made a full-size copy on paper and pricked the lines with a pin. Then he laid the paper over the panel and dusted the holes with charcoal powder. When he lifted the paper away, a fine outline was left behind.

Next came the paint. Slowly, with almost invisible brushstrokes, Leonardo and Andrea built up the scene in thin, delicate layers. To start with, they used fast-drying, egg-based paints. But for the final touches, Leonardo switched to oil paints, which took ages to dry.

Oil paints suited Leonardo's painstaking style. He could spend days on even the tiniest details, trying to perfect every fold of cloth and curl of hair. In fact, he spent so long on his angel that he began to get bored.

"Maybe I should leave this for a while and try something else?" he suggested.

Andrea frowned. "Finish what you're doing first," he warned. So Leonardo kept at it – with amazing results.

"If you keep painting like that, you'll put me out of business!" Andrea joked proudly when he saw the finished picture.

Detail from *The Baptism of Christ* – the picture Leonardo helped Andrea to paint. Leonardo's angel is the one on the left.

Leonardo's skills grew as the years passed. By his early twenties, he was one of Andrea's top assistants, working on picture after picture, while younger boys ground his pigments and cleaned his brushes.

He was always busy. When he wasn't painting, he would spend hours drawing. He filled whole notebooks with sketches of faces and landscapes, ideas for mechanical toys, notes on science and new machines – whatever caught his interest…

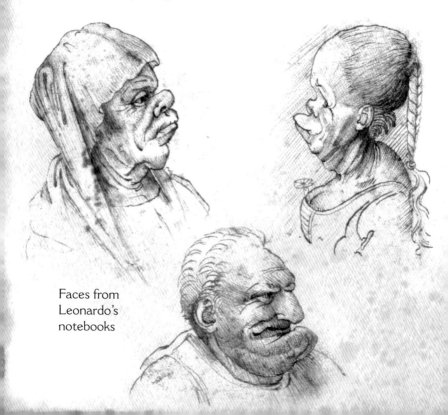

Faces from Leonardo's notebooks

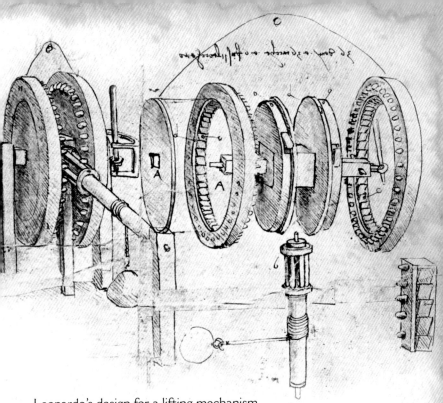

Leonardo's design for a lifting mechanism,
with gears to control its speed

Sometimes, when the mood took him, he
made up songs on his lyre (a stringed
instrument a little like a guitar). He just
couldn't stop his brain from buzzing – and he
was getting ready to move on.

On his 26th birthday, Leonardo took the
plunge and set up his own studio. He had
grown into a confident young man. It was
time to stretch his wings.

"If I don't try for myself, I'll never know," he told his old master.

Andrea nodded. "I understand," he said. He hesitated, then added, "Just one piece of advice, Leonardo – stick with things! Make sure you finish what you start."

Leonardo smiled uncomfortably. It was an echo of his father's words, all those years ago.

Now, Leonardo worked hard to establish himself. But, without Andrea's guidance, his natural impatience soon got in the way. His first order was for a painting in a chapel. He only got as far as a sketch before dropping the project. Nonetheless, more orders followed. Sometimes Leonardo finished them, sometimes he didn't – but he always charmed his clients into forgiving him.

Three years later, Leonardo was designing a new picture, an altarpiece for a local monastery. The sketches looked good, but his mind wasn't really on his work. His career wasn't going the way he wanted.

"There are too many artists in Florence," he muttered. "It's time to move on."

Leonardo's unfinished altarpiece, known as *The Adoration of the Magi*, showing the layout and first layers of paint. The young man standing in the bottom right-hand corner may be a portrait of Leonardo himself.

The Duke of
Milan's Castle

Chapter 3
Making it big in Milan
1482-1499

A few months later, Leonardo stood at the gates of another great city. Milan was 188 miles from Florence, and twice the size. To the ambitious 30-year-old Leonardo, it seemed full of opportunities.

Leonardo tried not to feel guilty about the half-painted altarpiece he had left behind. "One-off orders are all very well," he told himself. "But I need a patron – someone who will support me all the time, and who will appreciate my ideas as well as my art. Someone like Duke Ludovico…"

Ludovico, Duke of Milan, was one of the richest, most powerful men in Italy. He had already asked Leonardo to make a huge bronze horse. Now, Leonardo had come to persuade the duke to give him a full-time job. Leonardo made straight for the duke's castle.

In his hand, Leonardo gripped a letter he had written to give to the duke, in case he didn't manage to tell him everything in person…

My most illustrious Lord,

Sincere thanks for the order to build a bronze horse as a monument to your father.

I have other skills to offer Your Excellency and promise you I can make the following amazing things:

- *Portable bridges – fold them up and take them away.*
- *Cannon to fire a hailstorm of small stones.*
- *Cunning underground tunnels and winding passages.*
- *Indestructible war chariots – nothing can damage them.*
- *Catapults big enough to hurt grown men.*

Yours,   Leonardo

Stepping into the state rooms, Leonardo saw a dark-haired man sitting in a carved chair. Leonardo bowed.

"Leonardo!" exclaimed the duke. "Have you finished that bronze horse I ordered?"

Politely, Leonardo explained he hadn't begun it yet; he had been too busy inventing things. The duke listened closely as Leonardo reeled off idea after idea.

"I could use someone with your talents," he said eventually. "How would you like to stay in Milan and work for me?"

Leonardo grinned.

The duke kept Leonardo busy designing mechanical toys, costumes, weapons and buildings. But Leonardo still found time to take on a few other jobs. The first of these was a painting of Mary, Jesus, an angel and a young saint, for a chapel belonging to a religious brotherhood. Leonardo enjoyed making it – though he didn't follow his clients' orders at all.

"We asked for lots of angels. There's only one here!" said one brother crossly. "And why are they in a cave?"

Leonardo smiled. "I liked the mysterious look of it," he said.

In the end, the brothers accepted Leonardo's version. But Leonardo wasn't satisfied with it. He ended up painting a second version, which he gave the brothers a few years later.

Now Leonardo was a member of the duke's household, life should have been easy, but it was not to be. Ludovico was a powerful man, but he didn't have power to stop the plague – the deadly disease spreading through Italy.

Leonardo's first version of the painting, known as *The Virgin of the Rocks*

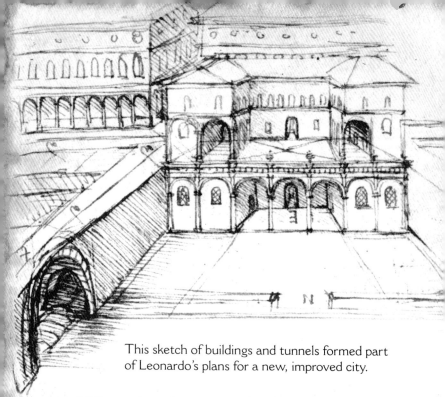

This sketch of buildings and tunnels formed part of Leonardo's plans for a new, improved city.

When the plague reached Milan, it killed over a tenth of the people in the city. The stench of rotting flesh became so bad, Leonardo began wearing perfume to block out the smell.

"How can the disease be stopped?" he wondered. He stopped painting and began drawing plans to improve hygiene in the city. He sketched out wide, clean streets, with new toilets and drains – though in the end, the disease passed and nothing was built.

Leonardo was much better at thinking and planning than getting things done. He was a dreamer. And his greatest dream was to fly. He loved watching birds and sometimes bought caged birds in the market, just to set them free and watch them fly. If he saw an eagle soaring, he would ask himself, "Could I do that?" And he would brush everything aside and start to sketch...

Leonardo's design for a winged glider

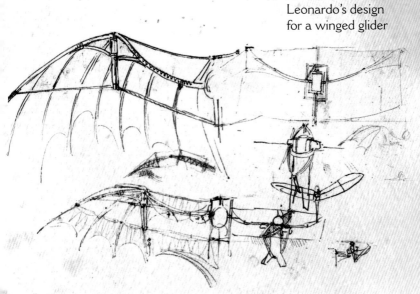

Despite all his plans, Leonardo would never be able to build a working flying machine. The right, lightweight materials were just not available.

But one project Leonardo did pull off was an awe-inspiring mural, or wall painting, in the dining hall of a Milan convent. Called *The Last Supper*, it shows Jesus and his disciples eating their final meal together.

Leonardo was obsessed. Sometimes, he worked from dawn to dusk without stopping. He was also trying a new way of making murals. Most were done straight onto fresh plaster, so the paints (which had to be water-based) sank in and became part of the wall.

A close-up of *The Last Supper* today, after restoration

Leonardo preferred to use egg- or oil-based paints, but they needed an undercoat, making the surface more likely to flake – and to make matters worse, the wall suffered from damp...

"Isn't it starting to peel?" asked one visitor.

"It's nothing!" Leonardo insisted, waving his brush dismissively.

The mural was huge – twice as high as a man. By the time Leonardo climbed down off the scaffolding for the last time, everyone agreed it was one of his best paintings ever.

"You're a genius!" the townspeople told him as they gathered beneath it. Full of drama and emotion, it brilliantly captured the moment when Jesus announced he would be killed because one of his disciples would betray him.

But, as people stepped closer to peer at the details, they couldn't help noticing the new method hadn't worked. Even as Leonardo packed up his brushes, flakes of paint were already falling off the wall.

With so many jobs and interests, Leonardo had had little time to spare for the duke's bronze horse. It was ten years before he even finished a model of it – a gigantic clay beast, three times the size of a real horse.

Then he spent more years working out how to turn it into bronze. A statue that big would be a huge technical challenge – even if he could get hold of enough metal.

One day, Leonardo went to ask the duke about buying the bronze. To his surprise, Ludovico shook his head.

"It can't be done," he said, glancing at the soldiers guarding his door.

"I don't understand," Leonardo said. "You asked me to make this statue."

"That's right," sighed the duke. "But I couldn't have predicted this."

"Predicted what?" asked Leonardo.

Leonardo made hundreds of sketches and diagrams planning the great bronze horse. This is just one of them.

"War," replied the duke gravely. "We're going to war with France. We need all our bronze to make cannons."

Leonardo walked slowly back to his studio, wondering what to do. Milan had been his home for 17 years and he didn't want to leave; but he couldn't stay and watch the city be torn apart. Undecided, he packed his bags but lingered – until news came that the duke had been defeated. Then, as French arrows shattered the great clay horse, Leonardo fled.

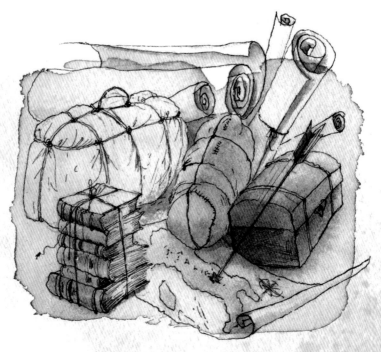

Leonardo's
sketch of
Isabella
d'Este

Chapter 4

Genius on the move

1500-1507

By now, Leonardo was nearly 50 and a
well-known artist and inventor. He could
have settled somewhere quiet and taken it
easy, letting his work come to him. But
instead, he decided to travel.

At Mantua, in eastern Italy, Leonardo
drew a sketch of the art-loving duchess,
Isabella d'Este.

Using just chalk and a few touches of pastel, the sketch was very simple and very beautiful.

Isabella was delighted. "Now you can get on with painting my portrait," she told Leonardo. "It'll be wonderful!"

"Later," Leonardo promised. In the meantime, he had other plans. As soon as the sketch was finished, he set off for Venice – a great Italian city built on a network of tiny islands.

Leonardo had been doing some thinking. These were dangerous times, with rival princes battling for control of different parts of Italy. Leonardo hated war, but he enjoyed the challenge of designing clever machines. He was full of ideas and prepared to offer them to anyone who would listen. He told himself he didn't mind what side they were on, as long as they allowed him to try out his inventions.

A view of Venice today, with many buildings and bridges unchanged from Leonardo's time

Leonardo went straight to the offices of the Venetian authorities.

"Look at my moveable dam," he told them. "You can use it to make a tidal wave to destroy your enemies." He pushed sheets of plans across the desk to a gloomy official.

"Too impractical," the official said, pursing his lips.

"Well, what about this submarine? Great for attacking enemy ships!"

"I don't think so," said the man.

Leonardo had one idea left. "You'll love my idea for a diving suit. It comes with an aqualung which lets you breathe under water. Amazing!"

The man shook his head. "It would never work," he said.

Leonardo shrugged. Obviously, his talents weren't appreciated in Venice. Stepping out into the fresh air, he came to another decision. "Back to Florence, I think," he told himself. "It's 20 years since I've been there."

So, a few days later, he was back on the road again.

Leonardo got a much better reception in Florence. The city's ruling family had been forced out, but there were still plenty of wealthy people wanting paintings. There was only one problem – he still had trouble finishing anything.

45

Leonardo's most important new order was a mural for the city's Council Hall. It was a grand project designed to celebrate a great battle. There was just one drawback – a young star named Michelangelo was doing a mural on the adjacent wall. The two artists disliked each other, and each wanted to prove *he* was best.

Leonardo planned a brilliant scene, full of rearing horses and desperate swordplay. It was a disaster. His paints wouldn't dry in the damp hall so he lit a fire, but that made things worse. Some of his paints set hard and others ran badly. In the end, he abandoned the project. Soon after, Michelangelo gave up too.

As if that wasn't bad enough, Leonardo was starting to get into trouble with other clients. Some local friars were chasing him for a new painting they had ordered, and Isabella d'Este was still waiting for her portrait.

The trouble was, Leonardo wanted a break from painting. So when a powerful duke named Cesare Borgia offered him a job as a roving military engineer, he jumped at the chance. He soon came to regret his decision.

Cesare was violent and ambitious, and trying to take over most of central Italy. Working for him wasn't easy. People who offended Cesare tended to be found later with their throats cut – even his own family.

When Leonardo visited Cesare's headquarters, he found the duke sitting stroking one of his pet leopards. His blue eyes narrowed as he watched Leonardo bow.

"Show me what you have," he snapped. "I want to attack Bologna."

Hastily, Leonardo unrolled a sheaf of papers. He showed Cesare the detailed maps he had made, then moved on to the weapons.

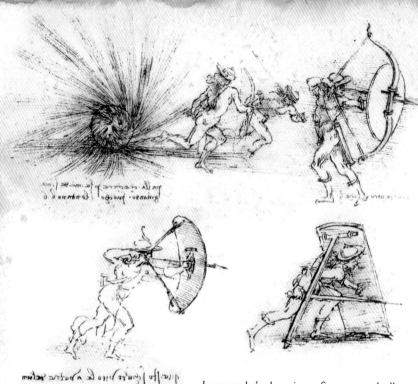

Leonardo's drawing of a cannonball
and different types of shields

"A tank with toothed wheels." Leonardo
showed Cesare the blueprint.

"That will definitely hurt," Cesare agreed.
"And?"

"A ten-barrelled cannon and a giant crossbow," Leonardo announced, pushing another
sheet of paper under Cesare's nose.

"Brilliant!" said Cesare, with a nasty smile.
"What else?"

"An adjustable cannon, catapults for hurling stones, a scythed chariot, a machine for storming walls..."

Cesare slapped Leonardo heartily on the back. "What a gruesome imagination you have!" he declared approvingly.

Leonardo smiled politely – but truth to tell, he was sickened by Cesare's bloodlust. Now, he longed to pick up a brush again. As soon as he could, he hurried back to his studio...

Leonardo's design for a giant crossbow

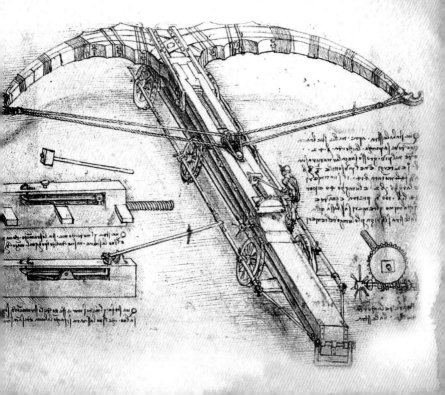

Close-up of
the *Mona Lisa*
by Leonardo

There, an order for a new portrait was waiting for him. The woman's name was not recorded, but legend has it she was a merchant's wife named Lisa. Gradually, on a small wooden panel, her face began to take shape. Leonardo spent ages trying to capture her modest half-smile. He got her to pose for days on end, hiring musicians and jesters to entertain her.

"You're making her look very mysterious," laughed one of the jesters.

It took Leonardo four years to finish the portrait – now known as the *Mona Lisa* – and he was very proud of it. In fact, he liked it so much that he kept it for himself.

In the meantime, the situation in Milan had settled down. The city remained under French control and had a new French governor, Count Charles d'Amboise. The Count wanted Leonardo to return to work for him. Cesare's battles were going badly; now would be a good time to leave. So, once again, Leonardo packed his bags.

Chapter 5

Anatomy uncovered

1508-1519

Back in Milan, Leonardo was as busy as ever. He worked as a painter, architect, town planner and water engineer. He designed beautiful pleasure gardens for his new French patron, the Count. He also became very interested in anatomy.

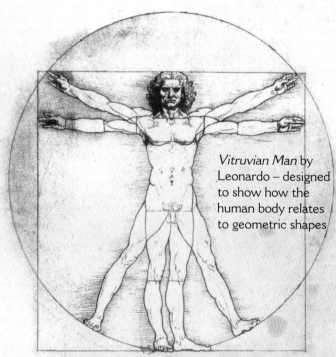

Vitruvian Man by Leonardo – designed to show how the human body relates to geometric shapes

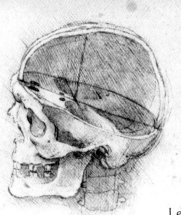
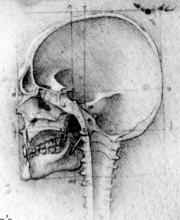

Leonardo's
studies of skulls

"In order to draw the human body, I need to understand exactly how it works," Leonardo explained to a doctor at the local hospital. "That means dissecting bodies."

"You'll need a special permit from the magistrates," the doctor told him.

Leonardo hurried to get a permit and start work. He dissected more than ten corpses, including the bodies of a hundred-year-old man and a two-year-old boy. It wasn't pleasant work. And not everyone approved of corpses being cut up, even with a permit. Sometimes he had to work late at night, to avoid insults from local townspeople.

Then, after a few years, the Count d'Amboise died. Leonardo had lost his patron.

There was fighting in Milan, too; armies from Spain, Rome and Venice had arrived to try to drive out the French. The city no longer felt like a safe place to be.

Fortunately for Leonardo, Giuliano de Medici offered him a job in Rome. Giuliano was wealthy and well connected – he was the brother of Pope Leo, the head of the Catholic church. Gratefully, Leonardo accepted.

There were plenty of other artists in Rome. Leonardo's old rival Michelangelo was there, basking in praise for a vast mural he had done on the ceiling of the Pope's chapel. And a rising star named Raphael was busy decorating rooms in the Pope's palace.

Leonardo was now in his sixties. His hair was turning silver and arthritis was making it hard to paint. He led a quiet life, concentrated on his drawing and scientific ideas, and let younger artists enjoy the limelight. Not that he had lost all his spirit...

"Meet my dragon," he said to courtiers at the Pope's palace one day. Grown men ran screaming from the room. Laughing, Leonardo picked up the small reptile he'd brought.

"It's only a lizard," he explained to the few people left. "I just tied on some silver wings and horns!"

A view of Rome today, looking across to the area known as Vatican City, where the Pope has his palace

Then, in 1516, Giuliano suddenly died. Yet again, Leonardo needed a new patron, and one was not long in coming...

Leonardo's fame had spread abroad. Now, the King of France offered him a job as "first painter, architect and mechanic of the king" – with a kingly salary to match. So, that summer, Leonardo crossed the Alps to France.

François, King of France, was in awe of Leonardo, the great artist. Whenever the king could spare time from affairs of state, he would come to talk with him.

François insisted on buying the *Mona Lisa*, which he hung in his bathroom. He gave Leonardo a handsome red-brick house in Amboise, with workshops, stables and gardens. In return, Leonardo set about planning a new palace for the king. But the plans never left the drawing board.

On April 23, 1519, Leonardo drew up his will. He knew he wasn't well. Nine days later he died, at the age of 67. King François was at his bedside.

Leonardo had been a genius of his age – a man of huge talent. His life was over, but the small boy from Vinci would inspire people for centuries to come.

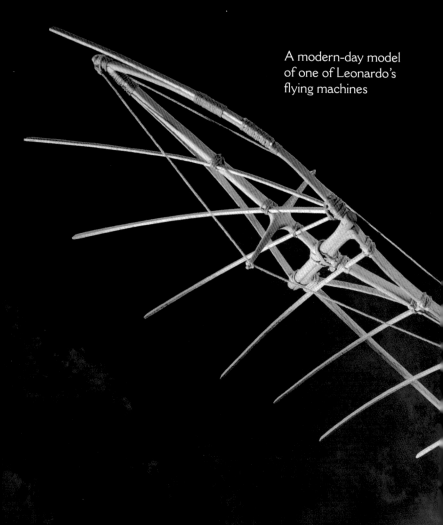

A modern-day model of one of Leonardo's flying machines

Even today, scientists marvel at Leonardo's notebooks. His observations of the world around him, his understanding of the human body and his ideas for new machines were far ahead of his time.

Art lovers flock to admire Leonardo's pictures, too. He left a dazzling wealth of drawings – over 4,000 in all. His paintings are much rarer. Of the few dozen he created, only 15 survive. But each one is a masterpiece, and the *Mona Lisa* is probably the most famous painting in the world.

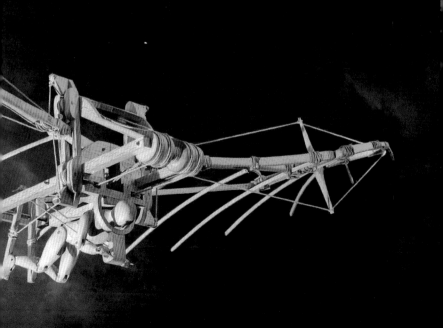

A page from one of Leonardo's notebooks. Can you spot a dragon among the cats?

My life as a genius

1452   I am born on April 15 near the village of Vinci.

1469   At 14, I go to Florence to work as apprentice to the amazing Andrea del Verrocchio.

1472   I become a member of the painters' guild of Florence. And I'm still only 20!

1478   I set up my first studio.

1481   I start work on an altarpiece for a local monastery. I just don't get around to finishing it because...

1482   I move to Milan to work for Duke Ludovico.

1483   I paint a picture of the Virgin Mary (now known as *The Virgin of the Rocks*) for a chapel in Milan.

1495   My biggest challenge yet – in a dining hall! I start the mural *The Last Supper* in a Milan convent.

1498   I finish *The Last Supper*, but the paint's already flaking off.

1499   Duke Ludovico falls from power, so I leave Milan for Mantua, where I sketch a portrait of Isabella d'Este, before moving on to Venice, and then back to Florence again.

1502   I'm employed as 'senior military architect and general engineer' by Cesare Borgia. What about that for a job title?

1503   I begin my battle mural for the Council Hall in Florence – though I never manage to finish it. But that upstart Michelangelo never finishes his mural either!

1503-5   I paint the *Mona Lisa*. You might have heard of it.

1513   I move to Rome, to work for Giuliano de Medici. I'm getting on a little now and arthritis is making it difficult for me to paint.

1516   The King of France invites me to come and work for him. He says he's my greatest fan!

1519   Sadly, Leonardo dies on May 2. But his name lives on...

Internet links

You can find out more about Leonardo, explore his studio and view more of his pictures, by going to the Usborne Quicklinks Website at **www.usborne-quicklinks.com** and typing in the keyword 'Leonardo'.

Please note that Usborne Publishing cannot be responsible for the content of any website other than its own.

Acknowledgments

Title page: *Presumed Self Portrait* © Bettmann/ CORBIS. **Page 9:** View of Vinci, Italy © James L. Amos/ CORBIS. **Page 13:** View of Florence, Italy © Michael S. Lewis/ CORBIS. **Page 23:** Detail of *The Baptism of Christ* (1472-75) © Summerfield Press/ CORBIS. **Page 24:** Details from *Five Studies of Grotesque Faces* © Galleria dell'Accademia, Venice, Italy/ The Bridgeman Art Library. **Page 25:** Facsimile of *Codex Atlanticus f.8v-b Transformation of Alternating to Continuous Motion: Design for a Two-Wheeled Hoist with a Caged Gear* (1503-07) © Private Collection/ The Bridgeman Art Library. **Page 27:** *The Adoration of the Magi* (1481-82) © Edimédia/ CORBIS. **Page 28:** Sforza Castle, Milan, Italy © John Stark/ Alamy. **Page 33:** *The Virgin of the Rocks* (1483-86) © Edimédia/ CORBIS. **Page 34:** *Architectural Sketch for an 'Ideal City'* © Bibliotheque de l'Institut de France, Paris, France, Giraudon/ The Bridgeman Art Library. **Page 35:** *Design for a Glider* © 2003 Topham Picturepoint/ TopFoto.co.uk. **Pages 36-37:** *The Last Supper* (1495-98) © 2002 Scala – Ministero Beni e Att. Culturali. **Page 39:** *Design for the Sforza Monument* © Alinari Archives/ CORBIS. **Page 41:** *Portrait of Isabella d'Este* (1499) © 1990 Photo Scala, Florence. **Pages 42-43:** View of Venice, Italy © Sergio Pitamitz/ CORBIS. **Page 50:** *Shields and a Cannonball* (1485-1500) © Alinari Archives/ CORBIS. **Page 51:** *Giant Catapult* (c.1499) © Biblioteca Ambrosiana, Milan, Italy/ The Bridgeman Art Library. **Page 52:** *Mona Lisa* (1503-05) © Gianni Dagli Orti/ CORBIS. **Page 54:** *Vitruvian Man* (c.1490) © Bettmann/ CORBIS. **Page 55:** *Skull Anatomy* (c.1489) © Mehau Kulyk/ SCIENCE PHOTO LIBRARY. **Page 56:** View of Rome, Italy © John and Lisa Merrill/ Corbis. **Pages 60-61:** Model of Leonardo's flying machine built by Andrew Ingham and Associates Ltd, photograph © Richard Waite. **Page 62:** *Cats and a Dragon* © Alinari Archives/ CORBIS.